KNOW IT ALL
FESTIVALS

By Louise
Nelson

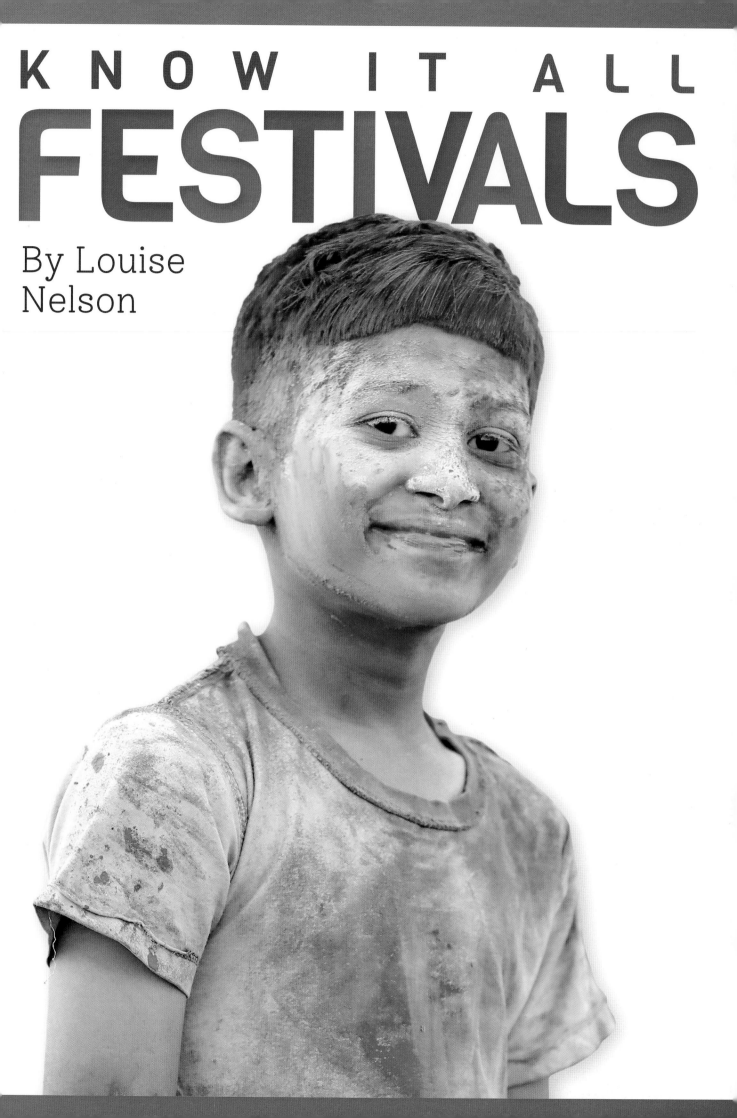

BookLife
PUBLISHING

©2021
BookLife Publishing Ltd.
King's Lynn
Norfolk PE30 4LS

A catalogue record for this book is available from the British Library.

ISBN: 978-1-83927-458-9

Written by:
Louise Nelson

Edited by:
John Wood

Designed by:
Dan Scase

All facts, statistics, web addresses and URLs in this book were verified as valid and accurate at time of writing. No responsibility for any changes to external websites or references can be accepted by either the author or publisher.

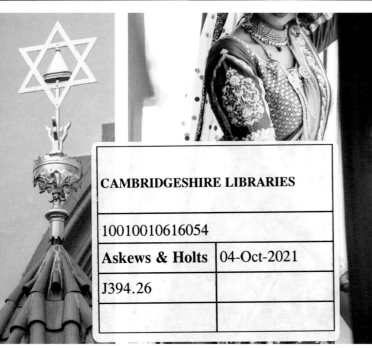

PHOTO CREDITS

All images are courtesy of Shutterstock.com. With thanks to Getty Images, Thinkstock Photo and iStockphoto.
Front cover: Silver Spiral Arts, Sofiaworld, BrAt82, Karan Daswani, Pavel Hlystov, BestStockFoto, Susan Schmitz, Vandathai, Please Remember, Alekcey, Pavel Hlystov, Alexapicso, OSABEE, ShaikhMeraj, siam.pukkato, NIKS ADS, BVFS. Page 4&5 – tomertu, Africa Studio, Rawpixel.com, Gold Stock Images, Sea Wave, wong yu liang, Evgeny Atamanenko. Page 6&7 – Love You Stock, chrisdorney, Rafael Dias Katayama, pujislab, Dinesh Hukmani, SantiPhotoSS, Akma Aripin, land_art, Vlada Young, Vova Shevchuk, agsaz, Pyty, saiko3p. Page 8&9 – Aliii, SyedAliAshraf, Rawpixel.com, Feroze Edassery, FamVeld, JeremyRichards, ixMaster. Page 10&11 – FamVeld, Romolo Tavani, Kristin F. Ruhs, szefei, hijodeponggol, Roberto Cerruti, tomertu, Romolo Tavani, Peter Titmuss, Doraemon9572, Pressmaster, Hugo Alejandri. Page 12&13 – Monkey Business Images, simona pilolla 2, wavebreakmedia, Pixel Prose Images, Melinda Nagy, Iakov Filimonov, Tim UR, xiaorui. Page 14&15 – Jonathunder, 1000 Words, glenda, Killiman. Page 16&17 – Dariia Belkina, berni0004, Art Stocker, Renata Sedmakova, Rachata Sinthopachakul, Svitlana Martynova, Valentina Razumova. Page 18&19 – jamesteohart, MiSt21, JOAT, StockImageFactory.com, Indian Food Images, Dipak Shelare, Kristin F. Ruhs, StockImageFactory.com. Page 20&21 – GiDes Photography, phortun, R.M. Nunes, Fer Gregory, Dina Julayeva. Page 22&23 – Sarath maroli, StockImageFactory.com, JOAT, StarLine, michaeljung, JOAT, ZouZou. Page 24&25 – Will Rodrigues, tomertu, Roman Yanushevsky, Noam Armonn, tomertu, Mordechai Meiri, FamVeld, Fascinadora. Page 26&27 – Tinxi, Mr Pics, Harsev SIngh, ChiccoDodiFC, pardeep rajwansh, Prabhjit S. Kalsi, Prabhjit S. Kalsi, UrbanUrban_ru. Page 28&29 – HunterKitty, Peiling Lee, SCHAMIN, Taras Vyshnya, Iakovleva Daria, David Cohen 156, Lee Thomas Scott. Page 30&31 – nuwatphoto, marietta peros, Satao, BALARAJU KOTNALA, yochika photographer, Rebecca Fitzgerald, Kzenon. Page 32&33 – RamonaS, Valentyn Volkov, Stephen Finn, StockImageFactory.com, Patrick Poendl, Celestebombin. Page 34&35 – imagedb.com, Lisa F. Young, White bear studio. Page 36&37 – NIKS ADS, Monkey Business Images.

CONTENTS

Words that look like <u>this</u> can be found in the glossary on page 38.
Key ideas you will need can be found on page 6.

FESTIVALS AND CELEBRATIONS

ALL TOGETHER NOW

Think of some of your favourite times of the year. Perhaps you're thinking of pretty decorations, exciting fireworks, delicious food or opening presents. Chances are, you're thinking of a festival.

Festivals are events where a **community** comes together and has a celebration. Festivals can be held to mark:

A religious event

A special day

A special event

A season

Roast turkey is a <u>traditional</u> food eaten at Christmas.

Beautiful red lanterns are used to celebrate Chinese New Year. Red is considered a lucky colour.

Festivals are often fun days. Special food, music, decorations and traditions all help to mark the days as important, and you might have time off school or work to take part. Festivals give us something to look forward to, and time to celebrate our **<u>culture</u>** with other members of our community.

Do you dress up and put up decorations for Halloween?

KEY IDEAS

RELIGION

Many people follow a religion. A religion is a shared set of **beliefs** and ideas about people and their relationship to a god or gods. There are many different religions in the world. The biggest and most well-known religions include:

ISLAM

BUDDHISM

CHRISTIANITY

SIKHISM

JUDAISM

HINDUISM

THE LUNAR CALENDAR

A lunar calendar for 2021

2021

Unlike the calendars you are probably used to, the lunar calendar follows the cycles of the Moon, and many religions use lunar calendars to chart their special events. Judaism and Islam use lunar calendars.

The phases of the Moon

RELIGIOUS BUILDINGS

Most religions have special buildings where people can go to **worship** and celebrate festivals. Special **prayers** are said by religious leaders, special events take place, and songs can be sung. Sometimes special foods are shared by the community.

DID YOU KNOW?

China uses a calendar which is lunisolar – it uses both the phases of the Moon and the position of the Sun in the sky.

Hindus worship in a mandir.

Sikhs worship in a Gurdwara.

Christians worship in a church.

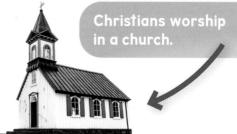

Jews worship in a synagogue.

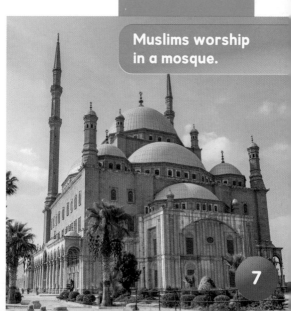

Muslims worship in a mosque.

LET'S CELEBRATE!

Whatever their beliefs, human beings like to mark special events or memories with a celebration. Festivals can mark happy events, like a day that is important to a country, or a day that is special to a certain religion. These days are often huge celebrations.

Many festivals are celebrated with exciting fireworks!

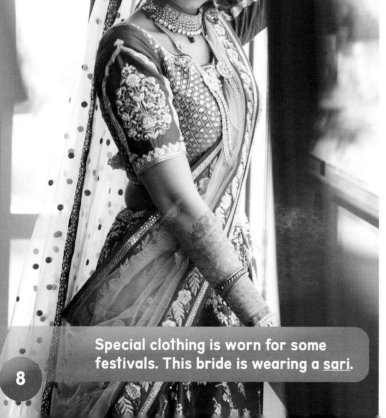

Special clothing is worn for some festivals. This bride is wearing a <u>sari</u>.

Delicious foods are often served at celebrations, such as this food for Eid.

8

Some festivals are very large, celebrated by millions of people around the world. Sometimes, nearly all the people in a country take the day off work and school so people can celebrate in their communities. Other festivals are smaller. Festivals can be held to mark all sorts of occasions.

A wedding is a festival for the friends and family of the couple getting married.

St Patrick's Day is a feast day celebrating Irish culture. It is celebrated by Irish people all over the world.

Independence Day is held in India every year to celebrate their __independence__ from Britain. There is a __parade__.

Because food is so important to people. lots of cultures celebrate a successful __harvest__ with a festival.

DID YOU KNOW?

Duanwu, or the Dragon Boat Festival, is held in China every year. People have been celebrating this festival for thousands of years!

TIMELINE: FESTIVALS

HANUKKAH

Jewish festival of lights

CHRISTMAS

Christian festival marking the birth of Jesus Christ

DHARMA DAY

Buddhist festival celebrating the first teachings of Buddhism

CINCO DE MAYO

Mexican national day celebrating Mexican culture and history

EASTER

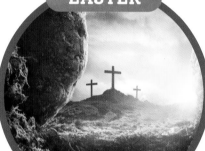

Christian festival marking the resurrection of Jesus Christ

HALLOWEEN

Traditional festival about all things spooky

DÍA DE LOS MUERTOS

This is the order that some festivals are usually celebrated in during a year. The dates of festivals might change depending on which calendar is used.

HOLI

Indian festival marking the **triumph** of good over evil in the Hindu religion

CHINESE NEW YEAR

PASSOVER

Passover remembers Moses leading the Jewish people from Egypt to freedom

VAISAKHI

Sikh New Year

MARDI GRAS

'Fat Tuesday' marks the end of Carnival with huge, colourful parades in the spring

Mexican festival remembering the souls of those who have died

DIWALI

Festival of lights marking the Hindu New Year

SECULAR FESTIVALS

Bonfire Night in the UK marks the anniversary of a failed <u>plot</u> to blow up the Houses of Parliament.

People who are not religious also like to celebrate – and many festivals are not religious at all. Festivals which are not to do with religions are called secular festivals. Many countries remember the end of wars with celebrations, sometimes for hundreds of years after. Others have national days that mark their independence or celebrate their country.

Music festivals bring together thousands of people to enjoy music and dancing.

Valentine's Day is a celebration of love.

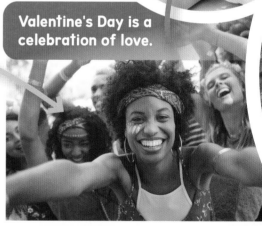

Celebrations to mark New Year happen all over the world.

Independence Day, or the 4th of July, marks the day the US became its own country.

Fun Christmas jumpers have nothing to do with Christianity. They are a secular tradition.

Some festivals are both religious and secular, or have become more secular over time. For example, Christmas is an important festival to Christians, but many people now also celebrate Christmastime without religion, seeing it as a time for family, gifts and treats. Many things we think of to do with Christmas are not religious at all.

DID YOU KNOW?

There is a festival in Spain called La Tomatina. Everyone in the town of Buñol has a huge tomato fight – just for fun!

CHRISTIAN FESTIVALS

ADVENT

Advent is the period leading up to Christmas. Advent is like a countdown to Christmas and it starts around the 30th of November.

An Advent crown is a special **wreath**. It has five candles which can often be seen in a church. One candle is lit for each Sunday before Christmas, and one for Christmas itself.

CHRISTMAS

Christmas celebrates the birth of Jesus Christ. The Christmas story tells how Mary and Joseph travelled on a donkey to Bethlehem, where Mary gave birth to Jesus, the son of God. **Wise** men and angels visited the baby and brought gifts and spread the good news of his birth.

The story of Mary, Joseph and the birth of the baby Jesus is often told in a play near Christmas. This play is called a Nativity play.

Some Christians attend a special <u>communion</u> service on Christmas Eve called Midnight Mass. <u>Hymns</u> are sung, and the churches are decorated.

Christians celebrate Christmas in church, where they sing songs celebrating the birth of Jesus.

LENT

Lent is the 40 days leading up to Easter. During Lent, Christians often give something up to remember how Jesus Christ went to the desert to **fast**.

The last day before Lent is called Shrove Tuesday. People often eat pancakes on Shrove Tuesday.

DID YOU KNOW?

The first day of Lent is called Ash Wednesday. Christians attend a special service in church, where they have a cross marked in ashes on their forehead.

16

EASTER

Easter is the most important festival to Christians. This festival celebrates the resurrection of Jesus Christ.

Maundy Thursday remembers how Jesus ate a final meal with his <u>disciples</u>. This is known as the Last Supper.

Good Friday is a day of sadness. Christians remember the day of Jesus's death on the cross.

Easter Sunday remembers the day Jesus rose from his <u>tomb</u> three days after his death. Christians call this the resurrection.

Eggs are used as a <u>symbol</u> of new life. to remember the resurrection.

Rangoli patterns are made from colourful flowers and powders.

HINDU FESTIVALS

DIWALI

Hindus pray to the goddess Lakshmi at Diwali, hoping she will bring them good fortune.

Diwali is the Hindu festival of lights. It takes place between October and November, depending on the lunar calendar. It lasts for five days. Diwali celebrates the story of how Prince Rama rescued Princess Sita from the evil king, Ravana. He was helped by Hanuman, the monkey god. The people lit a row of lamps to help them get home again. Diwali means 'row of lights'.

Diwali is a huge national celebration in India, with lanterns and fireworks!

Small lamps, called diyas, are lit to welcome Lakshmi to people's homes.

HOLI

On the first night of Holi, bonfires are lit to remember Prahlad's triumph over the evil Hiranyakashipu and his sister Holika.

Hindus celebrate the triumph of good over evil during Holi. Holi is a spring festival and marks the end of winter. The Holi story tells how Prahlad worshipped the Hindu god Vishnu, and not his father, the evil King Hiranyakashipu. Hiranyakashipu's sister Holika had special powers and tricked Prahlad into sitting in a fire with her, but Prahlad was protected!

The next day, colourful powders are thrown into the air.

Holi is celebrated by people all around the world.

DID YOU KNOW?

Holi is known as a festival of colours.

CASE STUDY: DÍA DE LOS MUERTOS

Día de los Muertos (the Day of the Dead) is a festival celebrated in Mexico on the 1st and 2nd of November. People believe the spirits of their dead loved ones return to spend time with them. Families create an ofrenda – an **altar** where they place bright flowers, sweets, bread, toys and other treats that their lost loved one might have liked.

An ofrenda in Mexico, decorated with candles and flowers

Calaveras are beautifully painted skulls. They can be <u>ceramic</u>, sugar or even painted onto a mask or as make-up!

Yellow marigolds are used to decorate ofrendas.

Día de los Muertos parade

MUSLIM FESTIVALS

RAMADAN AND EID-AL FITR

Ramadan is the ninth month of the Islamic calendar. It begins with the sight of a new crescent moon. Muslim adults fast during daylight hours, and spend time praying and doing good deeds. Ramadan ends with the festival of Eid-al Fitr.

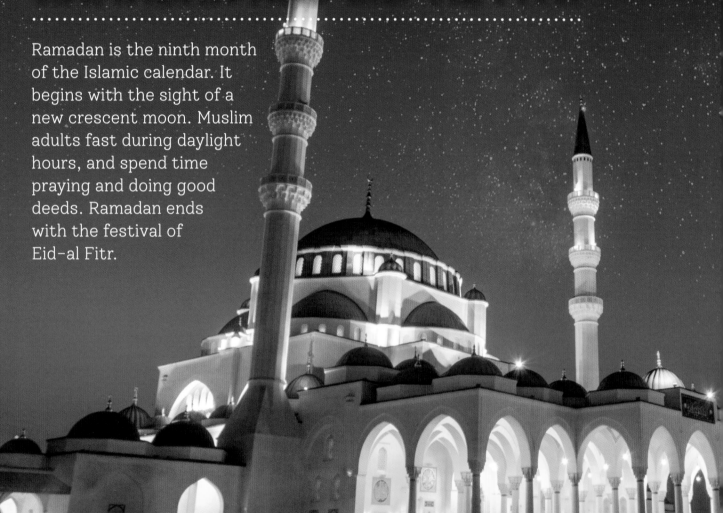

Eid-al Fitr is a celebration of the end of Ramadan. People thank <u>Allah</u> for helping them to be strong through fasting. Special prayers are said at the mosque.

Children receive presents, wear their best clothes and spend time with their families sharing food and celebrating.

Delicious foods are eaten at Eid-al Fitr.

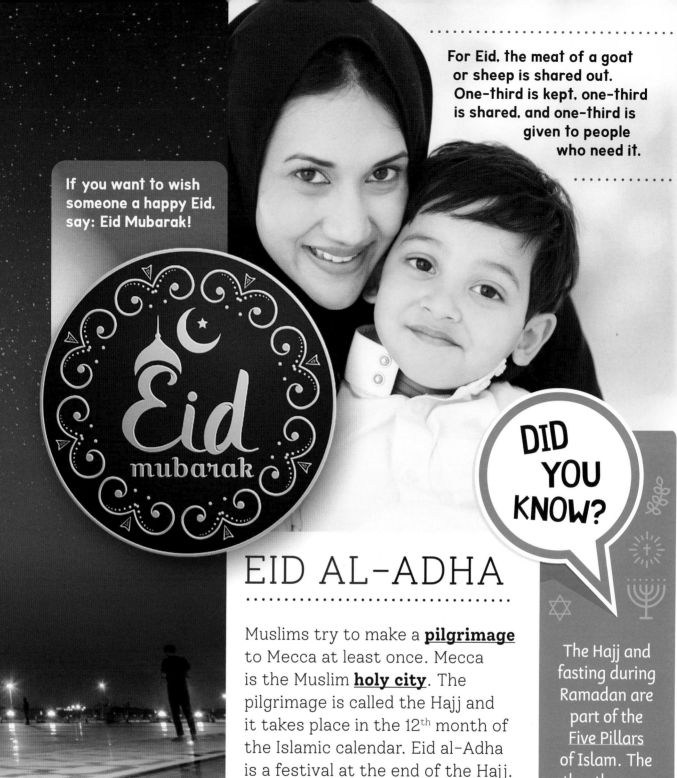

For Eid, the meat of a goat or sheep is shared out. One-third is kept, one-third is shared, and one-third is given to people who need it.

If you want to wish someone a happy Eid, say: Eid Mubarak!

Eid mubarak

DID YOU KNOW?

EID AL-ADHA

Muslims try to make a **pilgrimage** to Mecca at least once. Mecca is the Muslim **holy city**. The pilgrimage is called the Hajj and it takes place in the 12th month of the Islamic calendar. Eid al-Adha is a festival at the end of the Hajj.

The Hajj and fasting during Ramadan are part of the Five Pillars of Islam. The other three are declaring your faith, praying five times each day and giving money to charity.

Muslims go to a mosque for special prayers at Eid al-Adha. It is a time to visit family and friends and do good deeds.

PASSOVER

The Seder plate has five special foods. The foods are symbols of the Exodus story.

Passover remembers the Jews being led out of Egypt to freedom by Moses. This is known as the Exodus. The festival begins with a Seder – a special meal with prayers and **rituals** to help tell the story of the Exodus. The Haggadah is the book that this story is read from.

EGG

GREEN VEGETABLE

People sometimes sit on cushions during the seder, as a reminder that everyone is free and <u>equal</u>.

This is a matzah, a type of flat bread.

The Seder meal

MAROR (BITTER HERBS)

Hanukkah is the Jewish festival of lights. They light a candle for each day.

LAMB SHANK

Hanukkah lasts for eight days.

HAROSET
(a mixture including apples and spices)

HANUKKAH

Hanukkah tells the story of the Jewish people fighting to **defend** their right to believe in God. After the fight, they tried to light their special lamp, called a menorah, but they only had a tiny bit of oil left. By a **miracle**, the tiny bit of oil burned for eight days!

Foods fried in oil are served, to remind the people of the miracle of the oil lasting.

Games are played at Hanukkah and gifts are given. This special spinning top is called a dreidel.

SIKH FESTIVALS

The parade is led by five Sikh men in traditional clothing.

VAISAKHI

Vaisakhi celebrates the beginning of the Khalsa (the Sikh community) in 1699. The Sikh place of worship is called a Gurdwara, and it is decorated for Vaisakhi. There are parades, called Nagar Kirtan, and special food. Vaisakhi takes place in spring, usually around April 13th.

The Nagar Kirtan are very colourful and exciting!

Fireworks over the Gurdwara in Amritsar, India

This flag shows the Khanda, the symbol of the Sikh religion.

GURU HARGOBIND

BANDI CHHOR DIVAS

Bandi Chhor Divas celebrates the time the **Guru** Hargobind saved 52 princes from prison. The Emperor said only the men that could hold onto his coat could go free. But the Guru made a special coat, called a chola, with 52 **tassels** for them to hold, and they all went free.

Here, Guru Hargobind is freed from jail wearing his amazing tasselled coat, along with 52 Sikh princes.

Fireworks celebrate Diwali and Bandi Chhor Divas in India.

Bandi Chhor Divas is a festival of lights.

DID YOU KNOW?

Sikhs celebrate Diwali at the same time as Bandi Chhor Divas, and light lamps.

Much of the Western world celebrates New Year from December 31st to January 1st, marking the day the year changes. There are often fireworks, celebrations and parties in the streets.

NEW YEAR'S FESTIVALS

Chinese New Year falls between January 21st and February 20th. The Chinese New Year story says that a monster named Nian would attack at the start of a new year, but that Nian was afraid of lights, loud noises and the colour red. Each year, New Year is celebrated with those things, to scare off Nian.

The Jewish festival of Rosh Hashanah celebrates the new year. It begins in autumn. Rosh Hashanah takes place over two days. Apples and honey are eaten, to symbolise the new year being sweet.

Firework displays often bring in the new year.

New Year is a hopeful time to look back at the year that has passed and forward to the year ahead.

Hogmanay is the Scots word for New Year's Eve. Hogmanay is a huge celebration in Scotland, with fireworks and parties.

MORE FESTIVALS

The Yi Peng festival in Thailand usually takes place around November. Hundreds and thousands of bright lanterns are sent into the sky. It's the perfect time to make a wish for good fortune for the next year.

There are many beautiful and interesting festivals around the world. There are festivals about music, films, art and food. Here are a few more interesting festivals...

The Glastonbury music festival takes place in Somerset, England. Famous music artists come from all over the world to play.

In the town of Lewes in England, they take Bonfire Night very seriously. Each year, huge <u>effigies</u> are burned and there is a huge fire parade through the town.

In Japan, the Fuji Shibazakura festival celebrates the full bloom of the bright pink shibazakura flowers that grow near Mount Fuji.

In South Korea, the Boryeong mud festival is like a huge mud fight! People ski, swim, skid and slide in the mud, and there are muddy parties and fireworks!

DID YOU KNOW?

Oktoberfest in Germany has been called 'the world's biggest fair'. Traditional celebrations go on for two weeks, with fairground rides, parties and German food.

BELIEVE IT OR NOT!

Let's take a look at some weird and wonderful facts about festivals!

La Fête de la Fraise in France is a festival celebrating strawberries.

Each year in Huacho, Peru, they hold the Festival of the Guinea Pig!

The world's largest festival of the **performing arts** is held in Edinburgh each year. Performers of all kinds come from all over the world to present their shows.

More than 800 million people celebrate Diwali every year.

During the festival of El Colacho in Spain, newborn babies are laid on the ground in the street, and men dressed as devils jump over them. The jumping is supposed to clear the babies of any evil.

Harvest festivals are one of the oldest types of festival and are held all over the world.

ACTIVITIES

Can you complete these fun activities?

OUT AND ABOUT

Think of a festival you celebrate. Write a letter or speak to a friend and tell them all about how your family celebrates. Now ask them to tell you about a festival they celebrate. What traditions do you both have? What things do you do differently?

READ ALL ABOUT IT

Choose a festival you have found interesting, then see what you can find out about it. Create a fact file about this festival.

1. What is the festival called?

2. Where is the festival held?

3. When is the festival held?

4. What is the festival about?

5. What happens at this festival?

6. What special foods are served?

7. What special clothes are worn?

FESTIVAL WORDSEARCH

F	C	Q	H	J	S	A	A	T	P	A	D	R	V	M	Y	C	Y	X	D
A	H	W	D	P	F	Y	L	O	P	S	C	A	E	K	K	H	J	P	F
Y	I	E	Z	I	V	H	I	T	O	X	S	E	C	L	F	R	B	R	A
E	N	R	Q	A	W	U	L	S	L	F	W	T	G	M	H	I	F	J	E
H	E	T	P	I	A	A	E	T	K	U	E	Y	P	K	B	S	Z	B	N
P	S	Y	X	M	H	G	L	V	Y	A	P	O	J	L	A	T	S	N	K
Z	E	F	D	N	U	E	R	I	T	P	P	H	N	N	D	M	R	L	U
N	N	U	S	G	P	O	R	E	E	S	L	K	A	R	Z	A	V	M	D
Q	E	Y	Y	Q	A	R	B	E	G	L	I	U	W	N	C	S	I	C	X
T	W	E	R	W	S	G	T	W	E	E	J	L	D	D	U	L	O	V	G
Y	Y	B	F	Y	S	I	G	R	V	M	N	Y	R	S	R	K	P	W	F
B	E	O	W	D	O	E	V	A	I	S	A	K	H	I	W	P	K	E	T
D	A	N	E	S	V	H	T	G	S	D	E	H	A	W	P	K	L	A	L
P	R	F	L	L	E	X	B	Q	S	I	A	E	M	I	U	R	R	U	H
E	R	I	O	O	R	M	I	A	W	V	S	L	T	W	S	T	Y	O	A
G	R	R	O	E	E	A	L	P	E	Y	T	L	S	A	D	L	G	I	Z
U	F	E	O	Y	K	D	L	Z	N	E	E	O	I	K	F	O	S	E	S
I	A	H	O	L	I	D	Y	Z	K	N	R	I	T	M	F	I	Q	A	E
L	H	R	O	P	E	I	W	D	H	A	R	M	A	D	A	Y	H	L	M
S	P	K	L	Y	B	E	Q	E	G	L	H	M	N	G	M	B	G	J	P

Words to find:

Chinese New Year

Christmas

Diwali

Dharma Day

Hanukkah

Holi

Passover

Vaisakhi

35

QUICK QUIZZES

Can you remember the answers to all these questions? Check back through the book if you aren't sure.

1. Which food is traditionally eaten at Christmas dinner in the UK?

a) Turkey

b) Noodles

c) Cheese

2. What lucky colour are decorations for Chinese New Year?

a) Green

b) Yellow

c) Red

3. In which season of the year is Mardi Gras celebrated?

a) Summer

b) Spring

c) Winter

4. Which of these is a secular festival?

a) La Tomatina

b) Passover

c) Easter

5. Which of these is a secular Christmas tradition?

a) Midnight Mass

b) The Nativity story

c) Christmas jumpers

6. What do people throw on Holi?

a) Tomatoes

b) Fire

c) Coloured powders

7. Who is thought to visit on Día de los Muertos?

a) Loved ones who have died

b) Angels

c) Nature spirits

8. How do you wish someone happy Eid?

a) Eid Mumbai

b) Eid Monday

c) Eid Mubarak

9. How long does the oil burn for in the Jewish story of Hanukkah?

a) One day

b) Eight days

c) Fourteen days

10. How many princes did Guru Hargobind free from prison by making a special coat?

a) None

b) 25

c) 52

Answers: 1.a, 2.c, 3.b, 4.a, 5.c, 6.c, 7.a, 8.c, 9.b, 10.c

GLOSSARY

A

Allah the one and only God in Islam

altar a type of table, important for some religious services

B

beliefs strong opinions or thoughts on something

C

ceramic made of clay that has been hardened in an oven

communion a Christian service where bread and wine are shared

community a group of people who are connected by something

culture the traditions, ideas and ways of life of a group of people

D

defend protect, or make sure something isn't harmed or destroyed

disciples people who closely followed Jesus Christ

E

effigies big models of a person that are meant to be destroyed or burnt

equal when everyone is treated with the same amount of respect

F

(to) fast to not eat or drink, often for religious reasons

Five Pillars five rules or practices that all Muslims must follow

G

Guru a religious leader or teacher; in Sikhism, it is one of the first ten religious leaders

H

harvest the process of gathering crops

holy city a city that is thought of as important and sacred to a certain religion

hymns religious songs or poems in praise of God

I

independence being free and not controlled by anyone else

M

miracle when something amazing happens that cannot be explained

N

national day a day of the year for celebrating when a nation became a nation, or a day that is important to a leader of the country

P

parade when people walk or dance down a street with others watching

performing arts dance, music, poetry and other arts that are performed in front of an audience

pilgrimage a long trip or journey, usually to do with religion

plot a secret plan made by a group of people to destroy something or do something violent

prayers messages said to a god or gods, usually saying thank you or asking for help

R

resurrection a time when a dead person is said to come back to life

rituals actions and events that are done in a certain order, usually as part of a religion or belief

S

sari a long piece of silk or cotton draped around the body

symbol a thing that is used as a sign of something else

T

tassels knotted threads that hang from clothes, rugs and curtains

tomb an underground place for burying the dead

traditional to do with beliefs or actions that are passed down between people over time

triumph to win or overcome something

W

wise knowing lots of things

worship to show love for a god or gods

wreath a circle made of flowers and leaves

INDEX